Alon Bachar

Today I Did a Good Deed

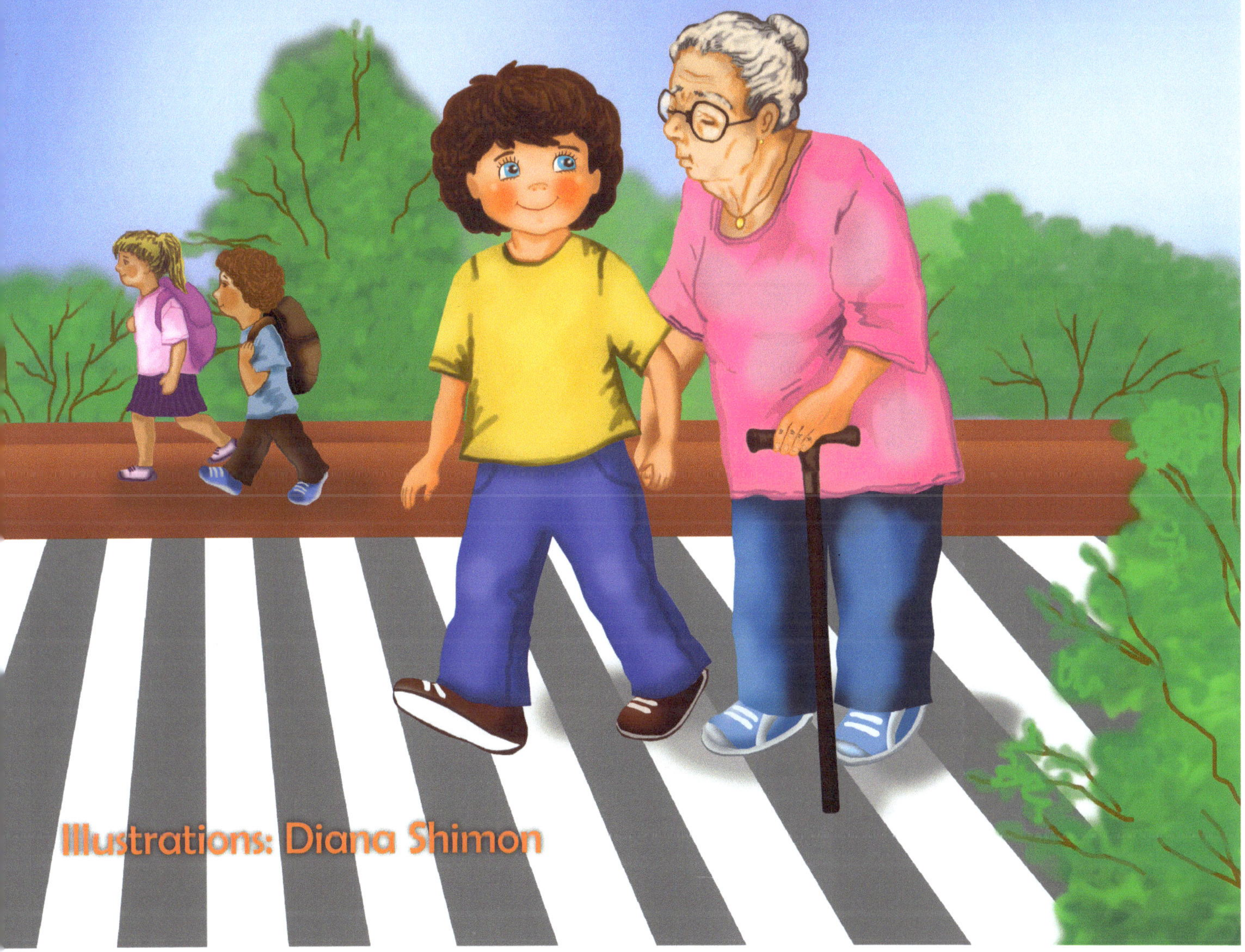

Illustrations: Diana Shimon

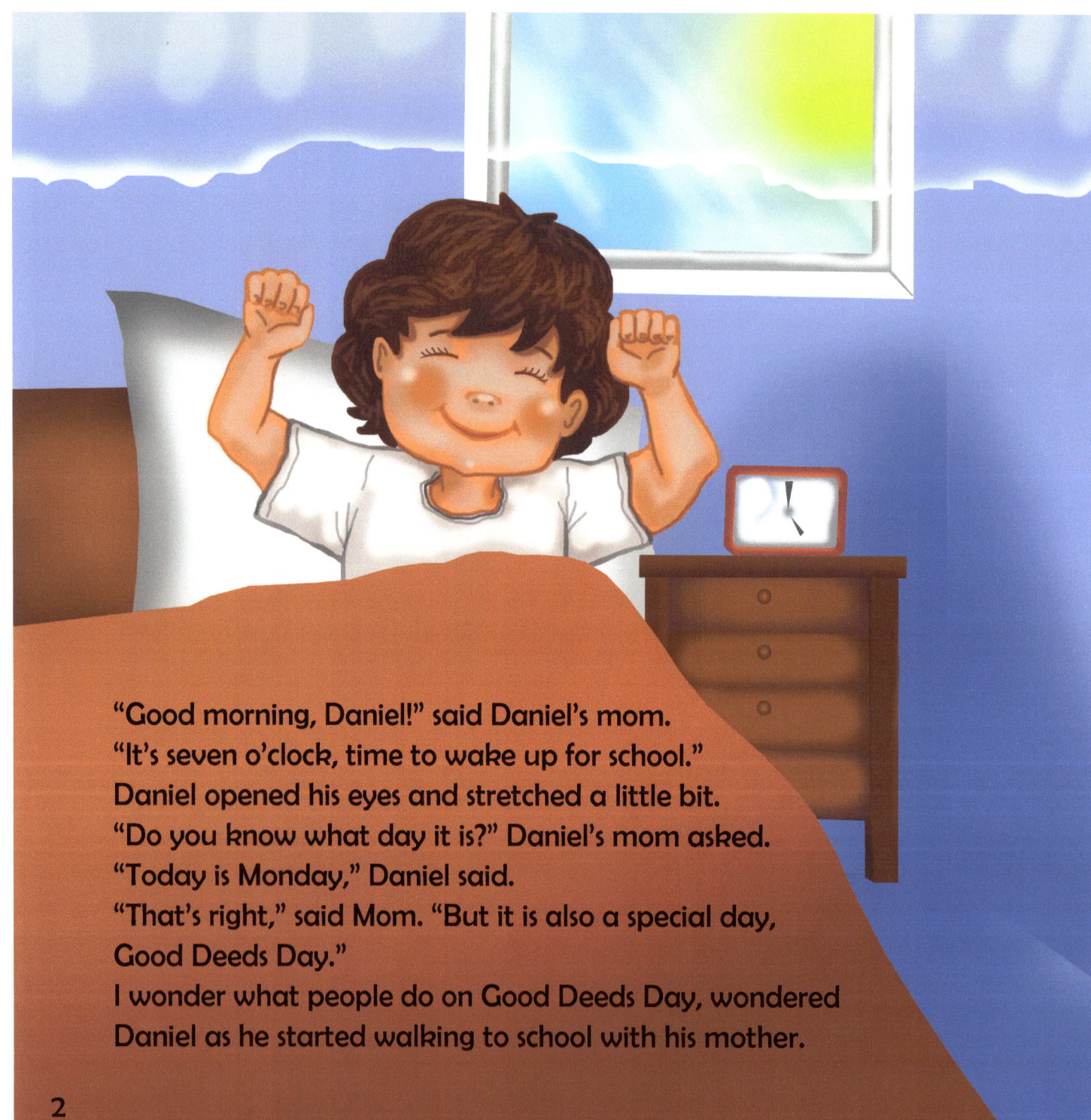

"Good morning, Daniel!" said Daniel's mom.
"It's seven o'clock, time to wake up for school."
Daniel opened his eyes and stretched a little bit.
"Do you know what day it is?" Daniel's mom asked.
"Today is Monday," Daniel said.
"That's right," said Mom. "But it is also a special day,
Good Deeds Day."
I wonder what people do on Good Deeds Day, wondered
Daniel as he started walking to school with his mother.

Daniel and his mom got to the crosswalk.
"Wait on this bench for one minute, right here," asked Mom.
"I will be right back, Daniel dear."
Daniel sat on the bench and looked at his mom.
She held an old lady's hand
and helped her cross the street.

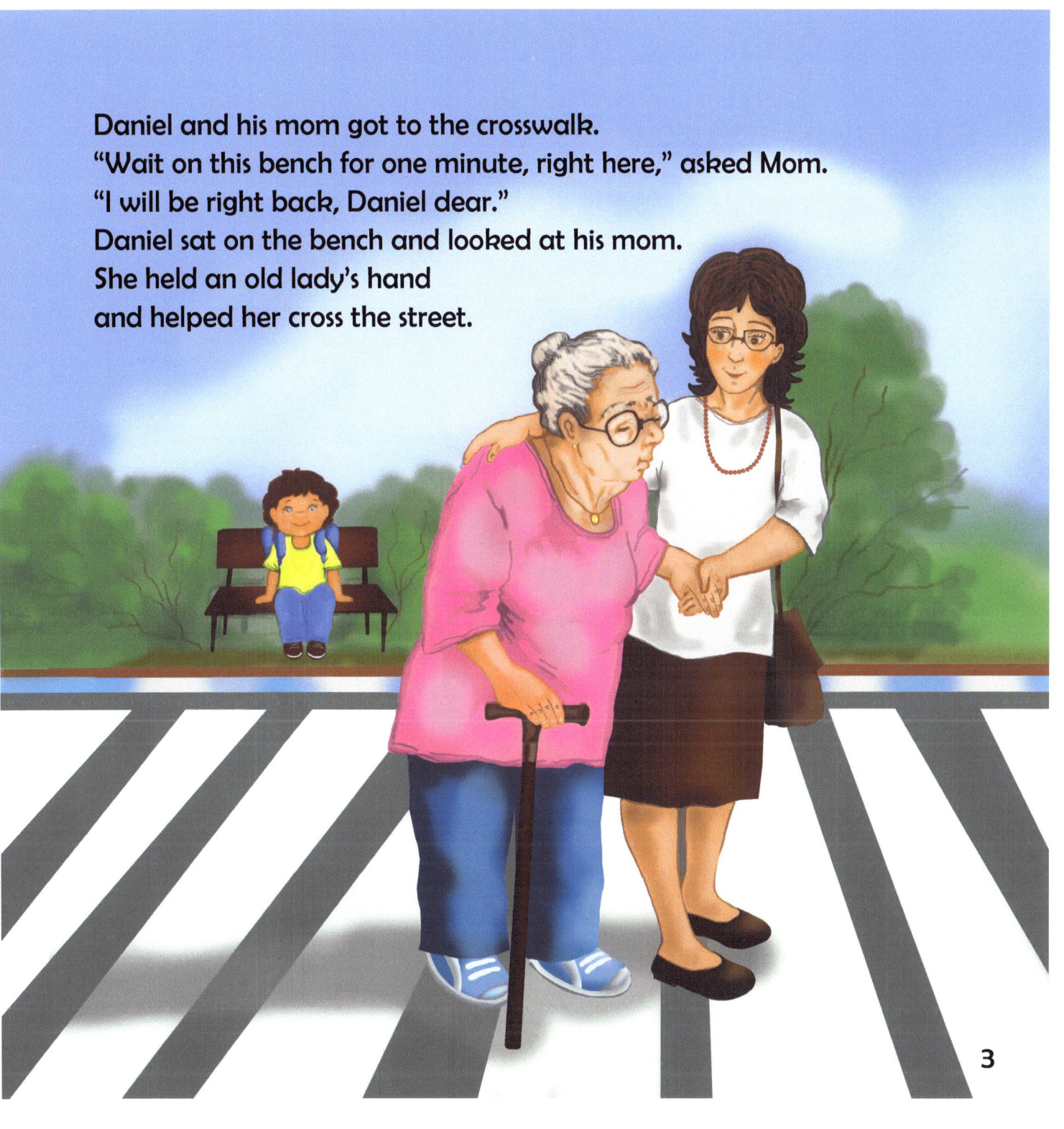

Mom walked back to the bench where Daniel was waiting,
and they both used the crosswalk to cross the street,
as they continued walking to school.
 "Who were you helping there?" Daniel asked.
"I don't think I know her."
"I don't know her either, but she can't cross the street alone,
so I helped her," said Mom.
"Today, I did a good deed."

"I want to do a good deed as well, Mom!"
Daniel asked.
Suddenly, they saw a cat.
The cat started yowling, meow meow!
"I think the cat is hungry," said Daniel.
"Should we get him something to eat?"
"Gladly," Mom answered.
"Let's go to the store and buy milk
and a treat."

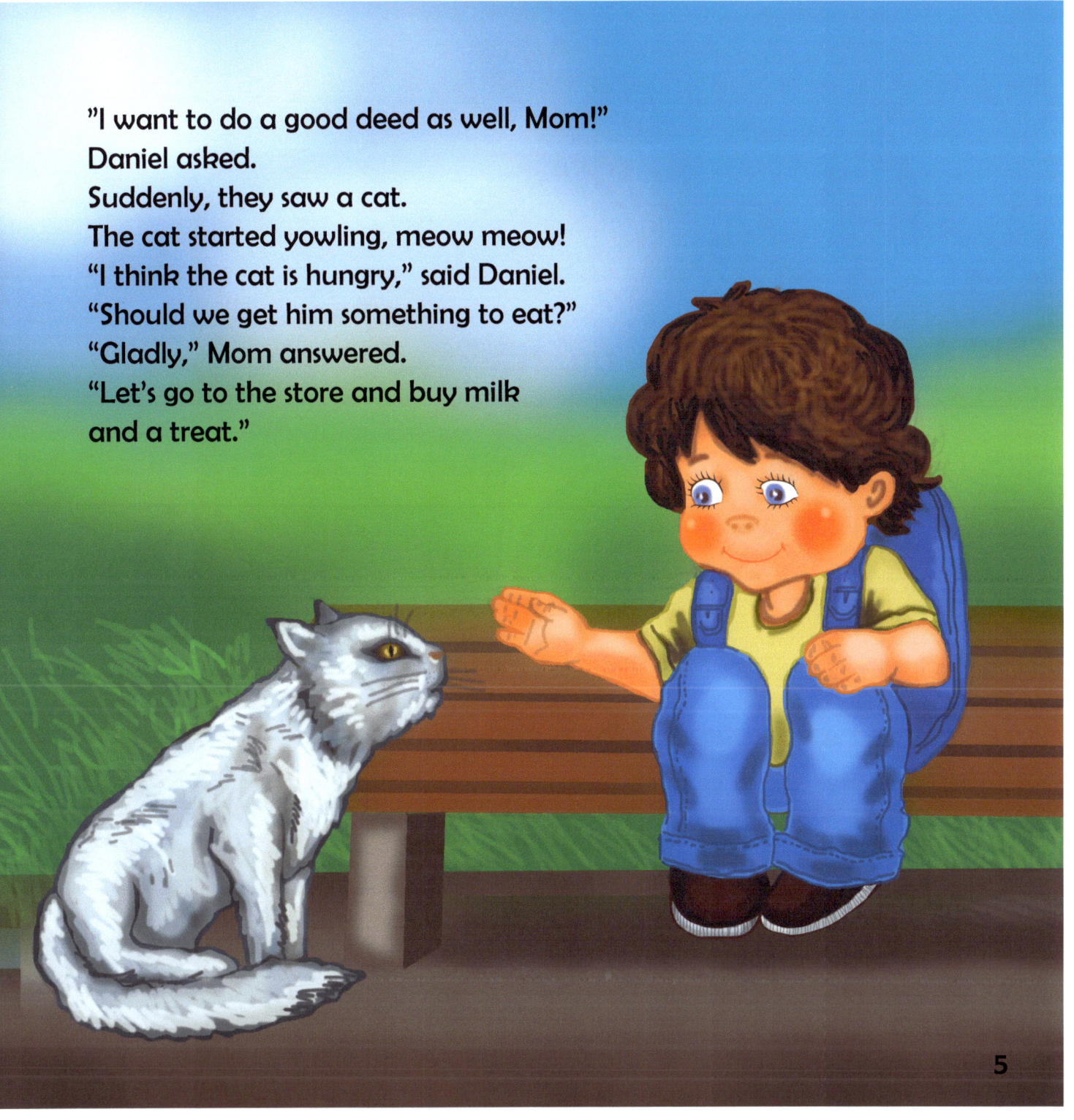

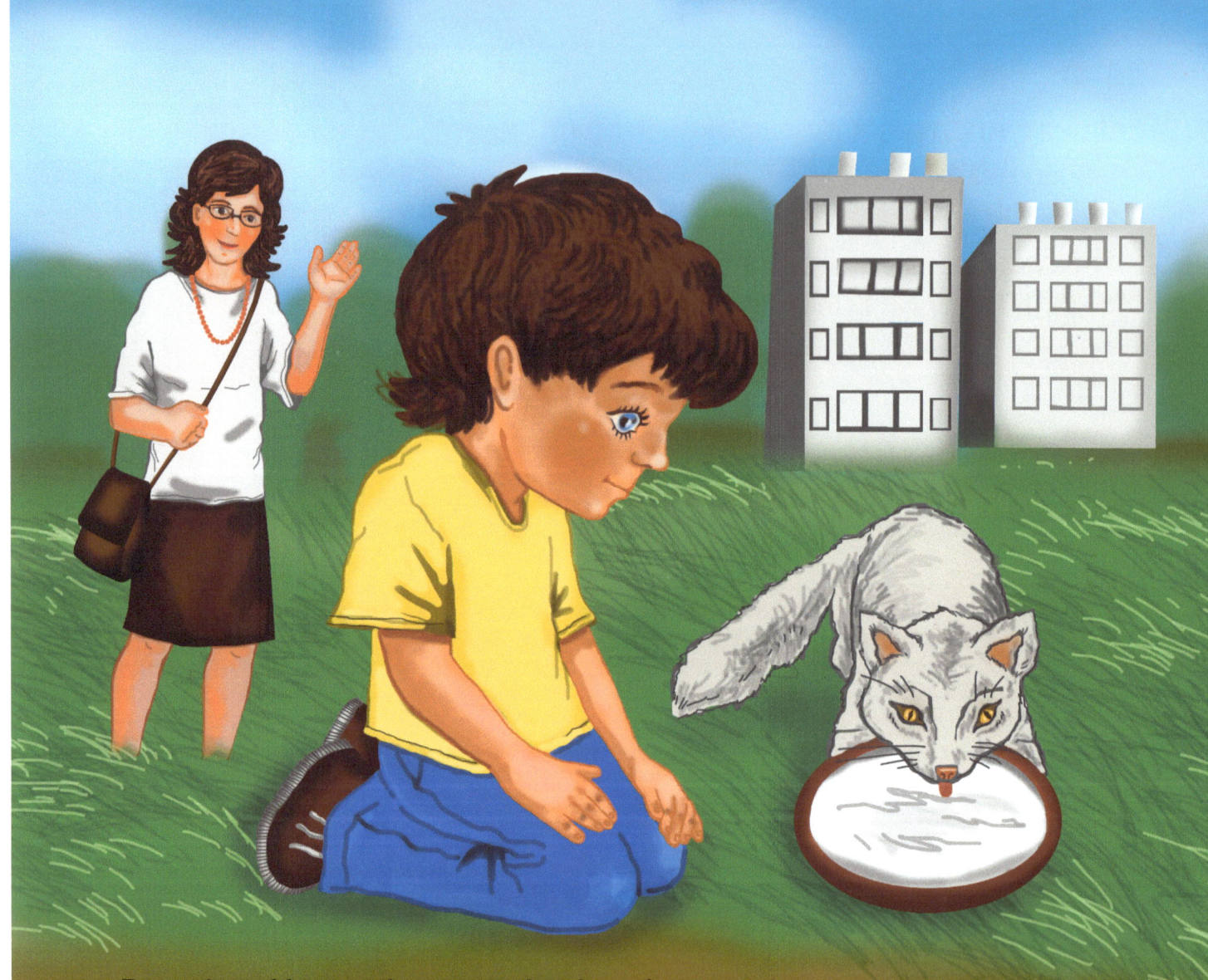

Daniel and his mother came back to feed the cat, and the cat enjoyed licking the milk from the bowl that was placed in front of him.

Mom said: "There you go Daniel, hooray!

You did a good deed today."

Daniel walked into the classroom with a big smile on his face and hurried to tell his teacher about the good deeds he and his mother did while walking to school.
Daniel's story warmed the teacher's heart.
She told the students proudly about Daniel and his mother's good deeds.

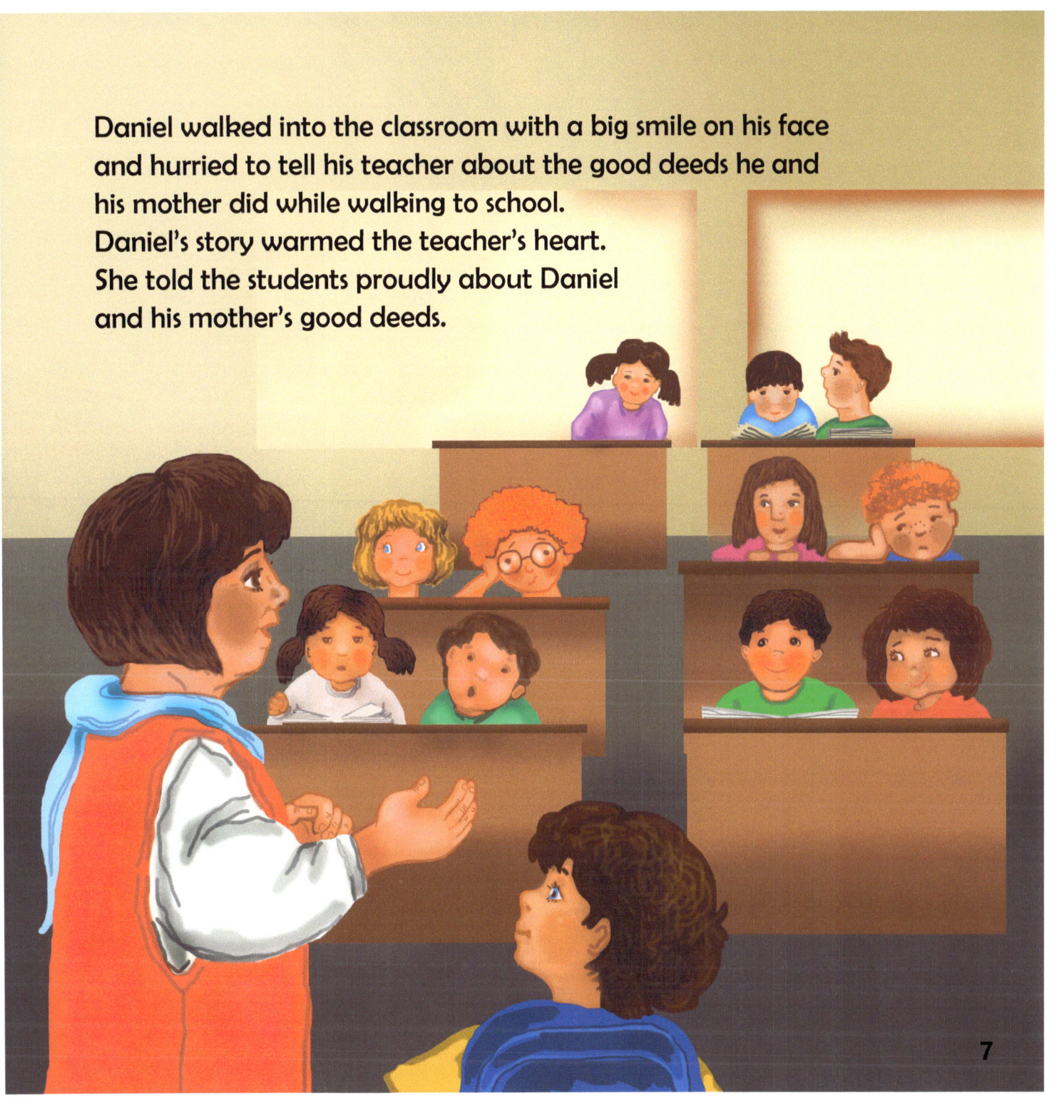

"We want to do good deeds too!" The students asked the teacher.
"Let's see... I have an idea!" the teacher said.
"Each student will receive a large trash bag.
During recess, you will pick up the trash
in the schoolyard."

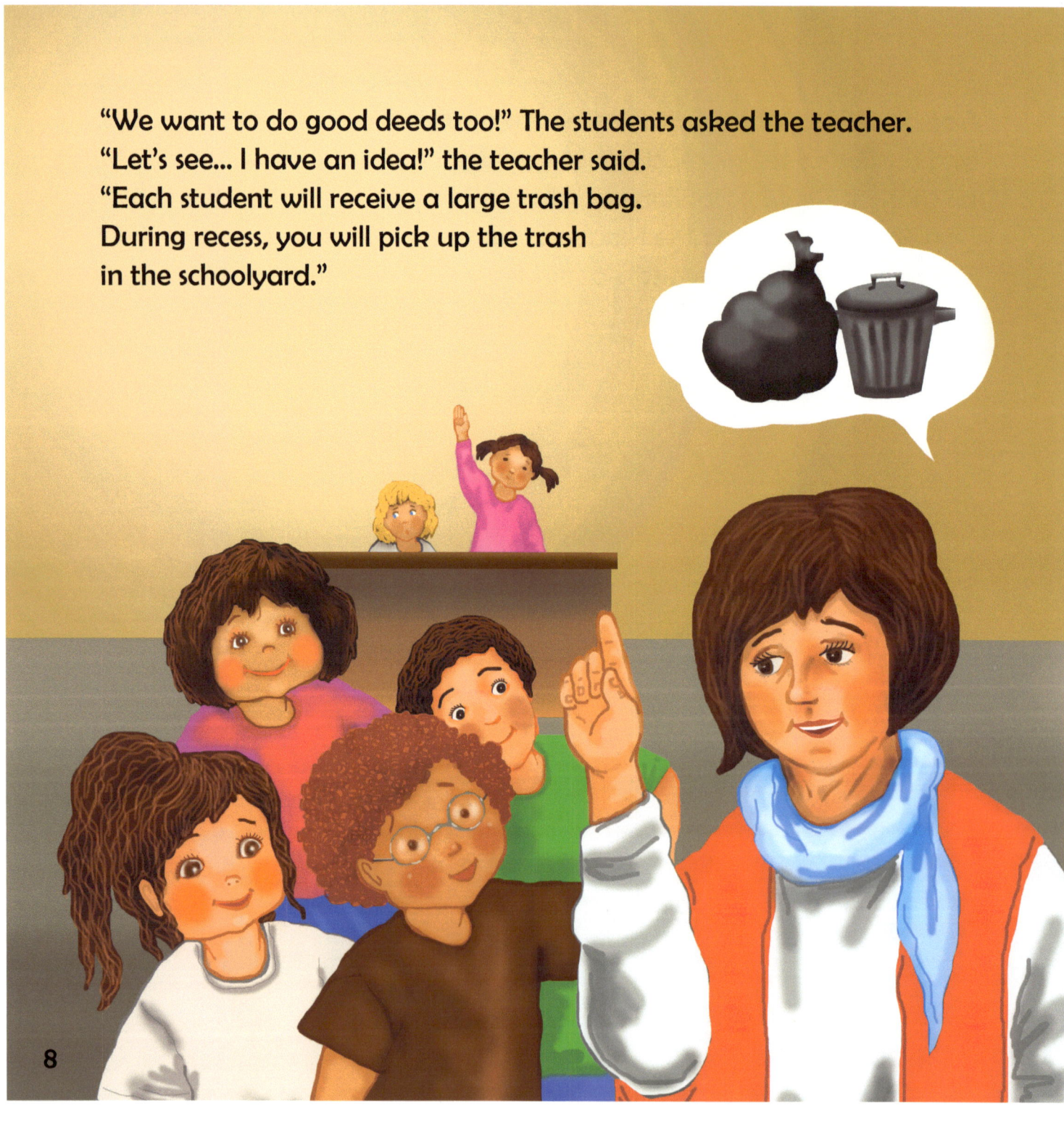

The school bell rang, and all of the students ran to the schoolyard and started cleaning it.

When the school principal got out of her office and saw how clean and organized the schoolyard was, she asked:

"Who cleaned the yard?"

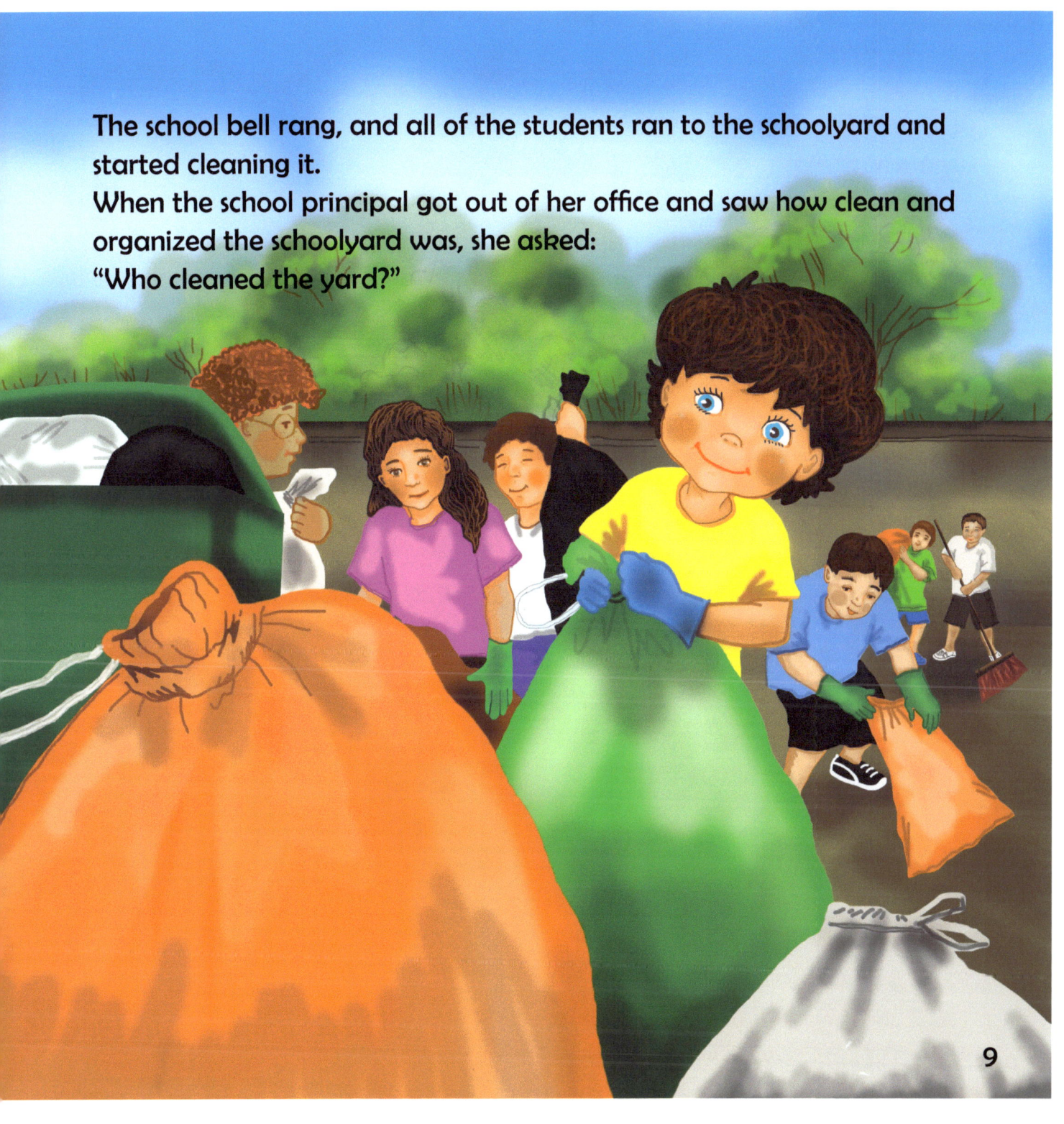

Daniel answered, "The entire class cleaned
the schoolyard.
We all worked very hard."
"Well done, students," the principal said.
"You did a good deed."

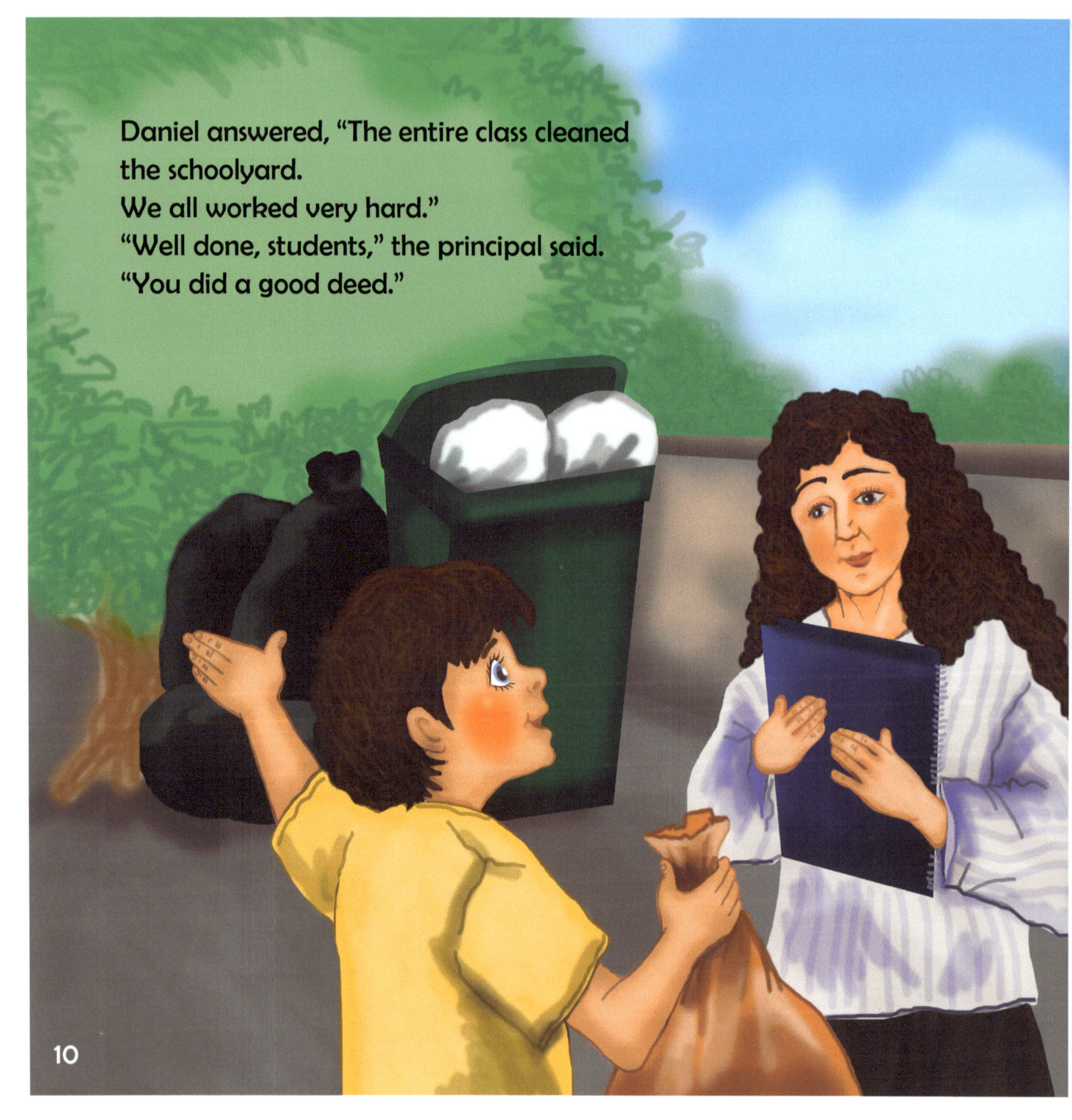

The school day has ended,
and Daniel started walking home.
He noticed a large container on the side of the street.
The words 'Bottles for Recycling' were printed on it.
Daniel kept walking and saw a weird trash can.
The words 'Paper for Recycling' were printed on the can.
Daniel scratched his head. I don't know what recycling is,
he thought,I better ask my mom.

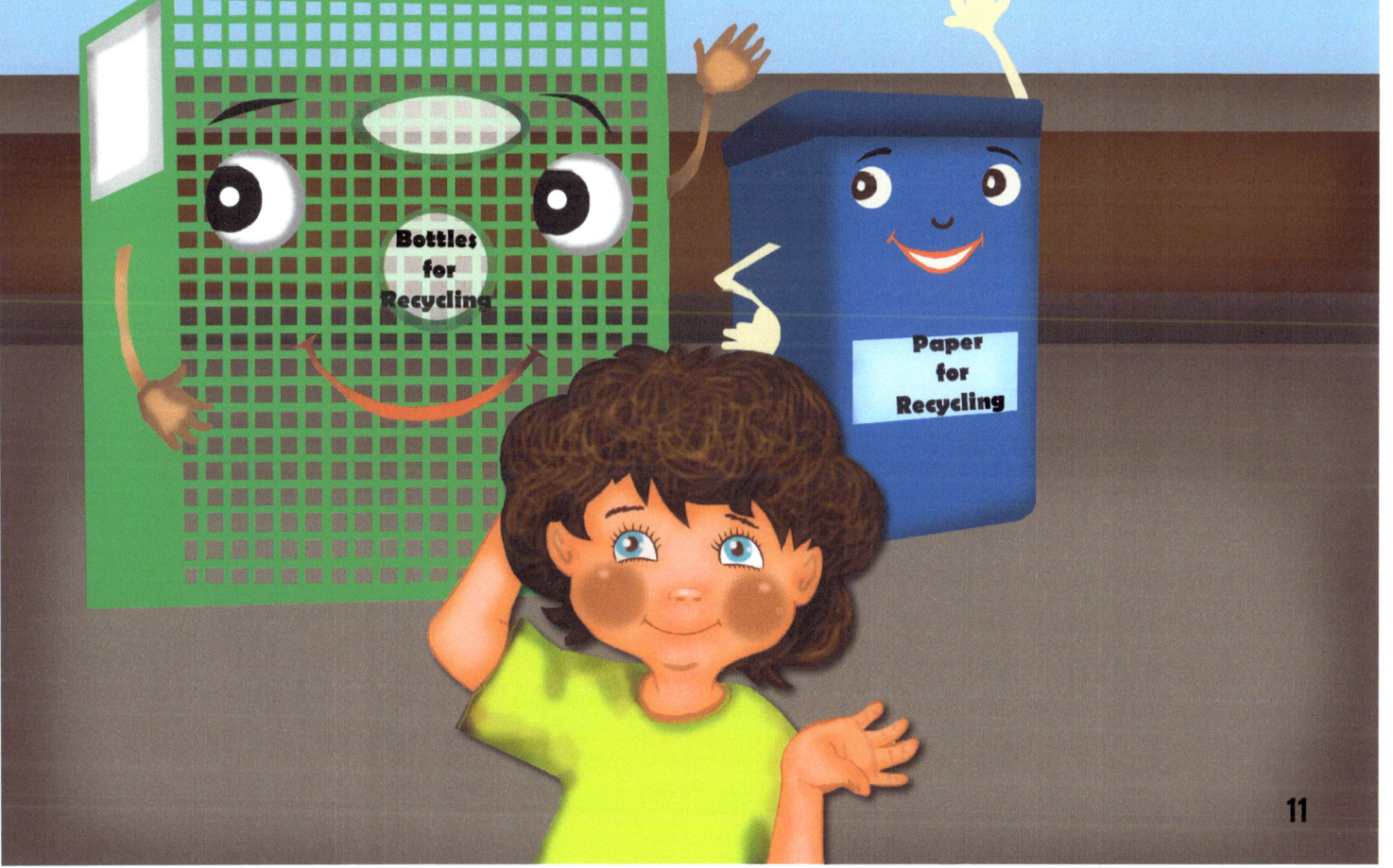

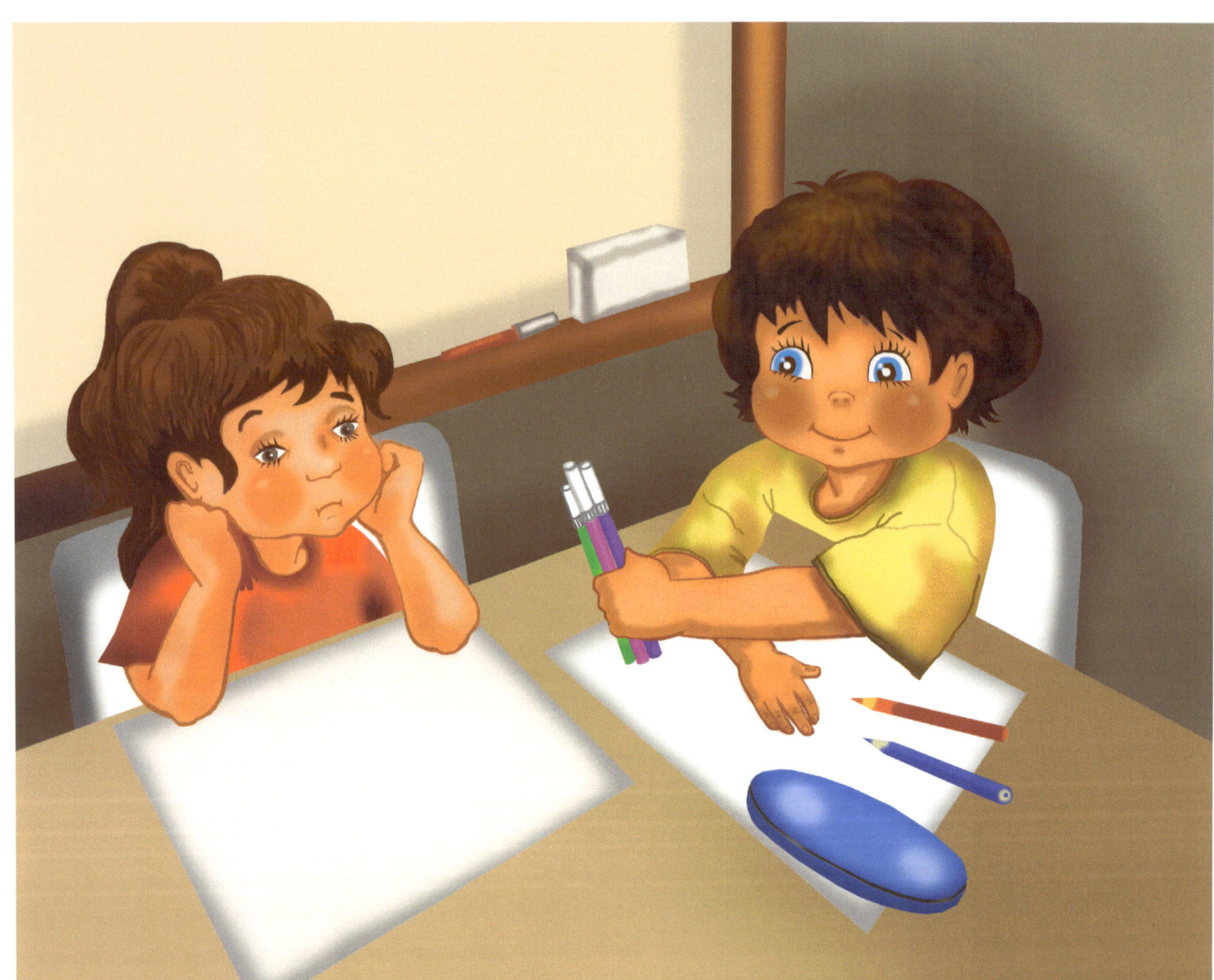

Daniel entered his house feeling very excited.
"Mom, today Noa forgot her pencil case for art class at home," he said.
"I noticed that she was very sad.
I gave her my crayons so that she will be glad."

With a shy smile, Daniel added:
"Noa made a drawing
and gave it to me as a gift."
"Well done, Daniel," said Mom.
"You did a good deed today."

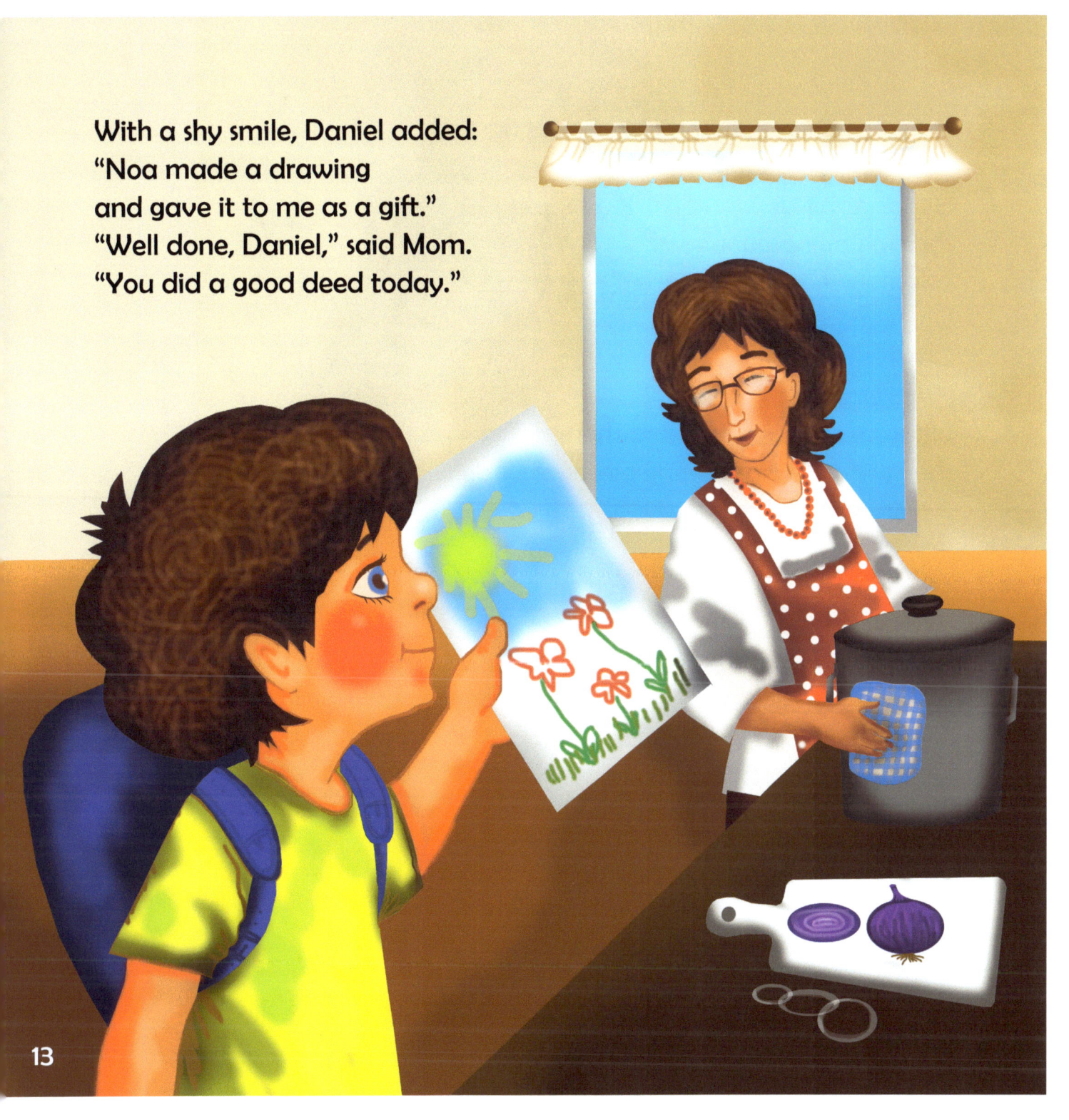

Daniel finished eating his lunch and hurried
to do his homework.
He sat at his desk and started flipping
through his notebook.
"Mom, how is paper made?"
Daniel asked.
Daniel's mom answered,
"Well Daniel,
big trees are cut down and then
they are made into many pieces of paper."

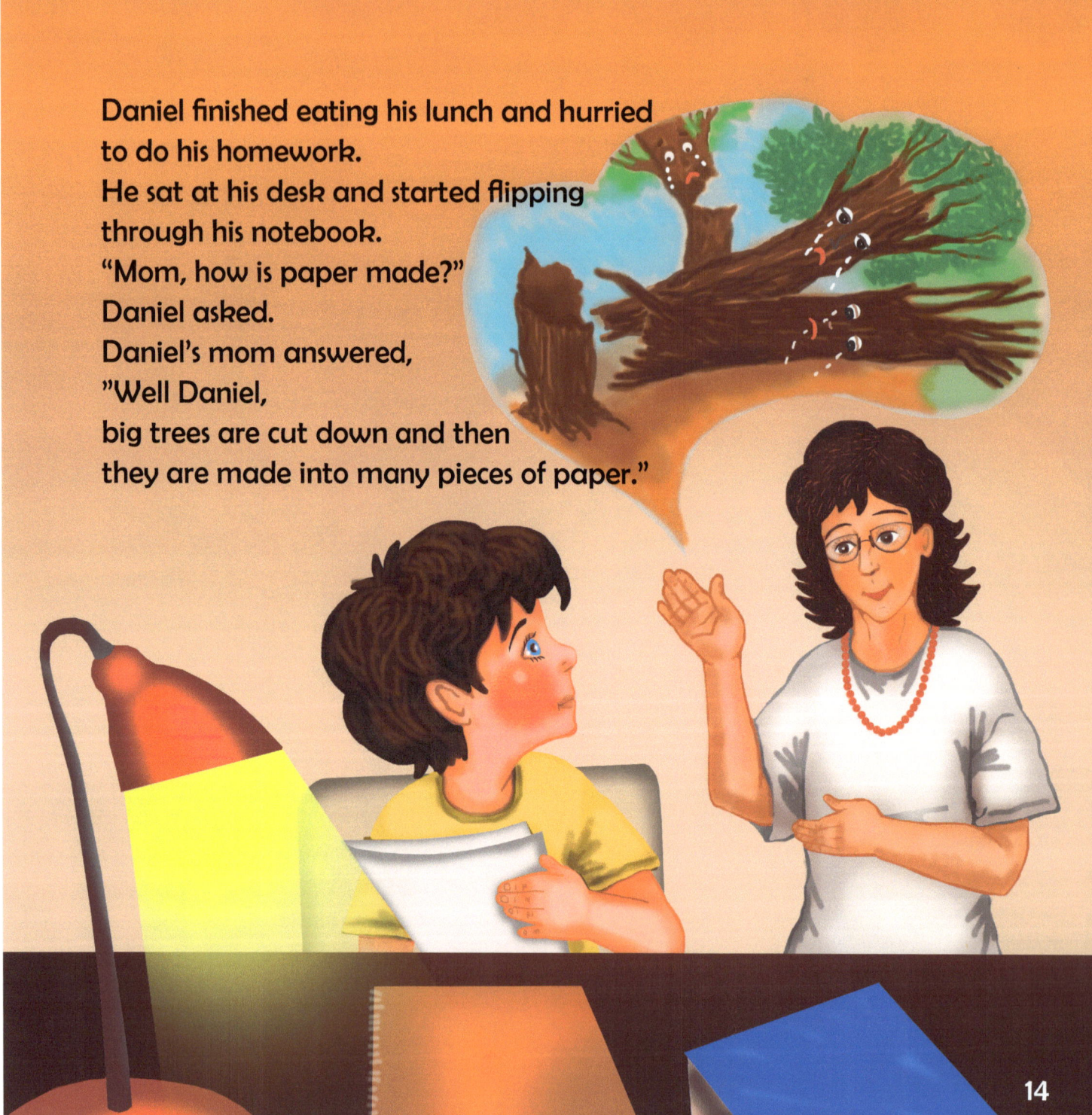

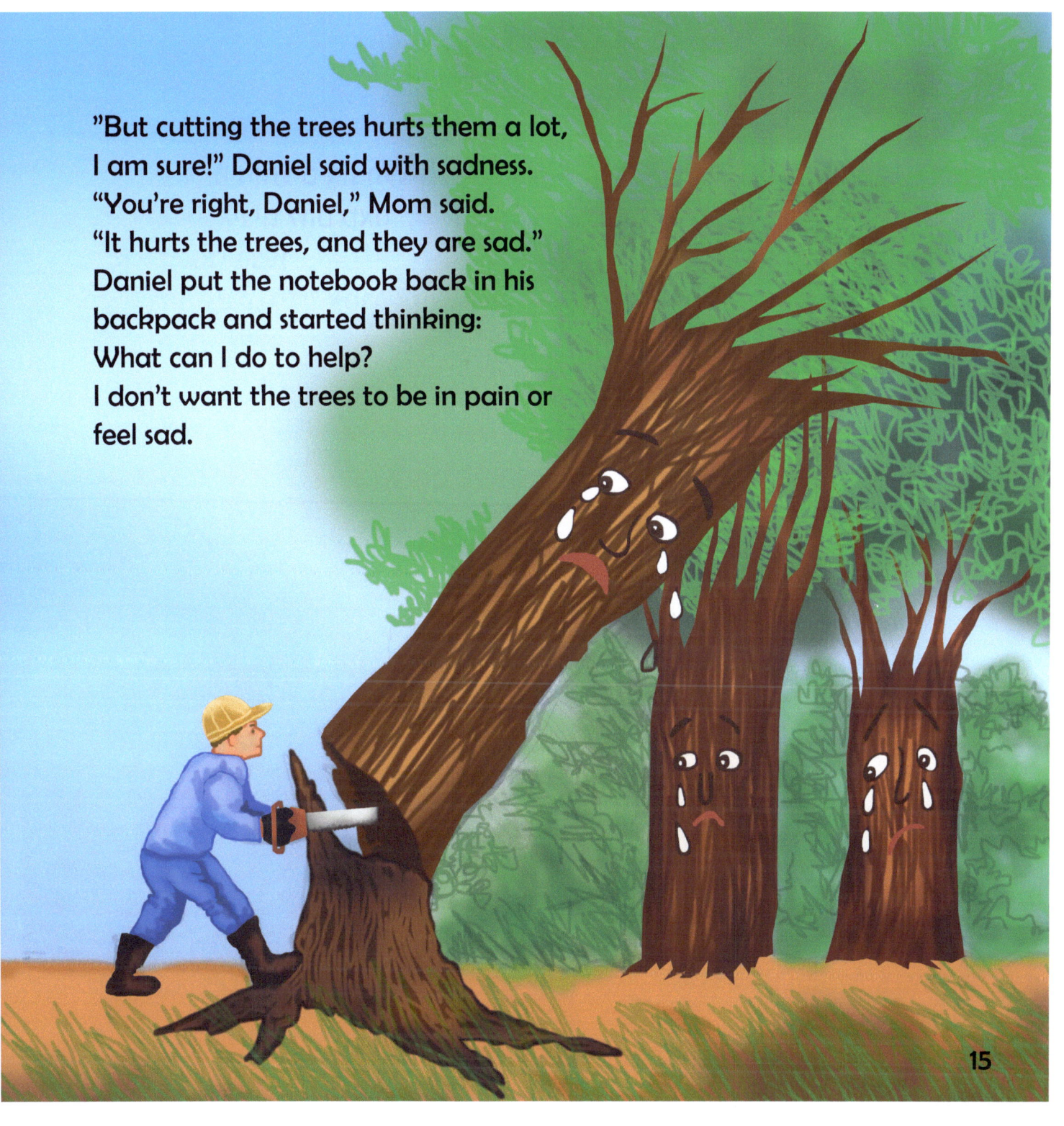

"But cutting the trees hurts them a lot,
I am sure!" Daniel said with sadness.
"You're right, Daniel," Mom said.
"It hurts the trees, and they are sad."
Daniel put the notebook back in his
backpack and started thinking:
What can I do to help?
I don't want the trees to be in pain or
feel sad.

15

"Mom, what is recycling?" Daniel asked.
"Recycling means creating something new from something old," Mom answered.
"In the factory, old bottles are used to create new ones.
Used paper turns into new paper and notebooks.
People throw away old things in the right recycling bin.
That way, we keep the environment clean.
Fewer trees will be cut down if we recycle the right way.
If we do that, the trees will smile every single day."

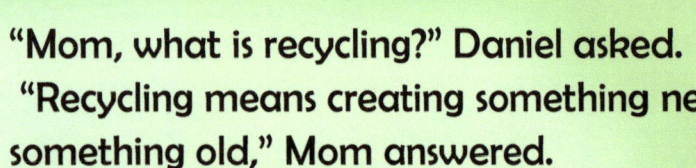

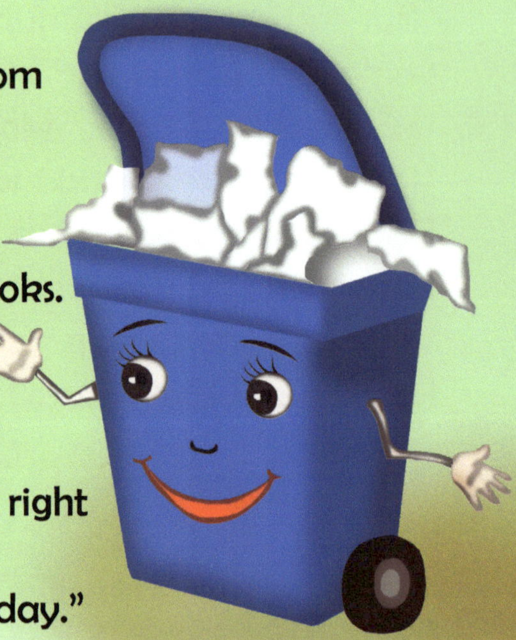

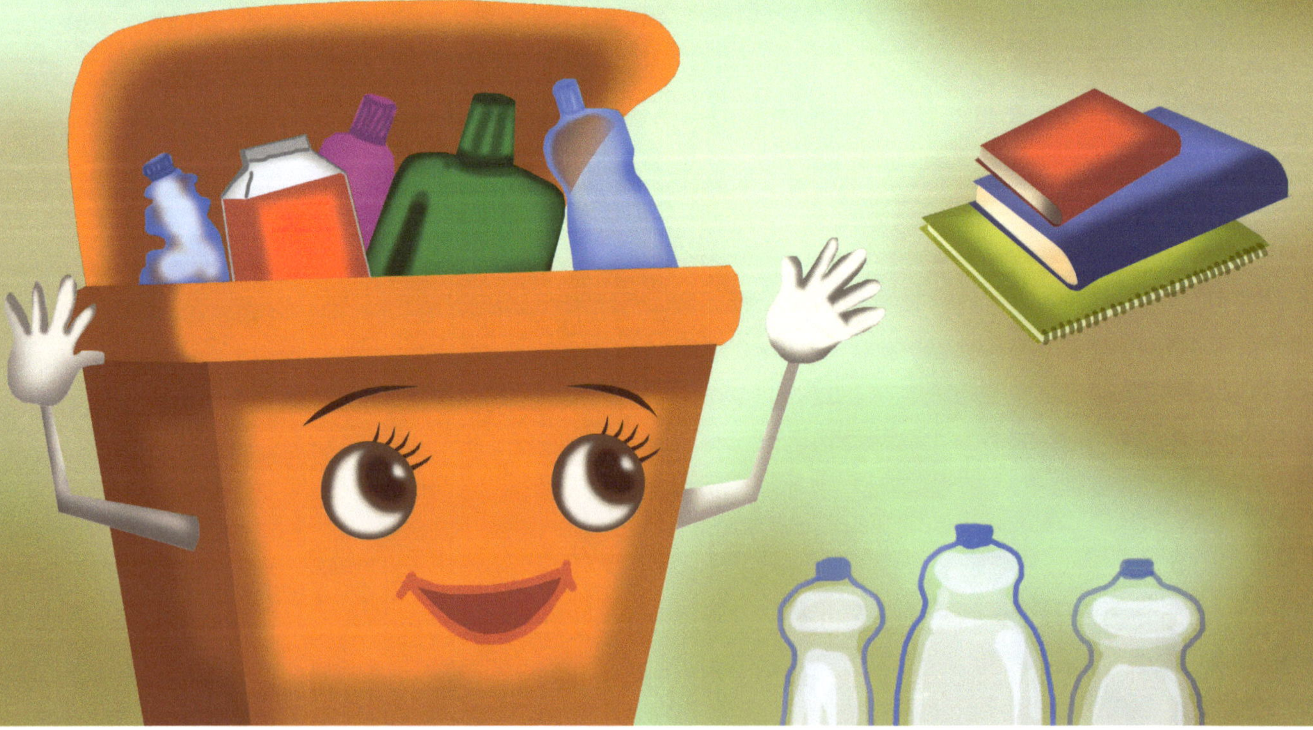

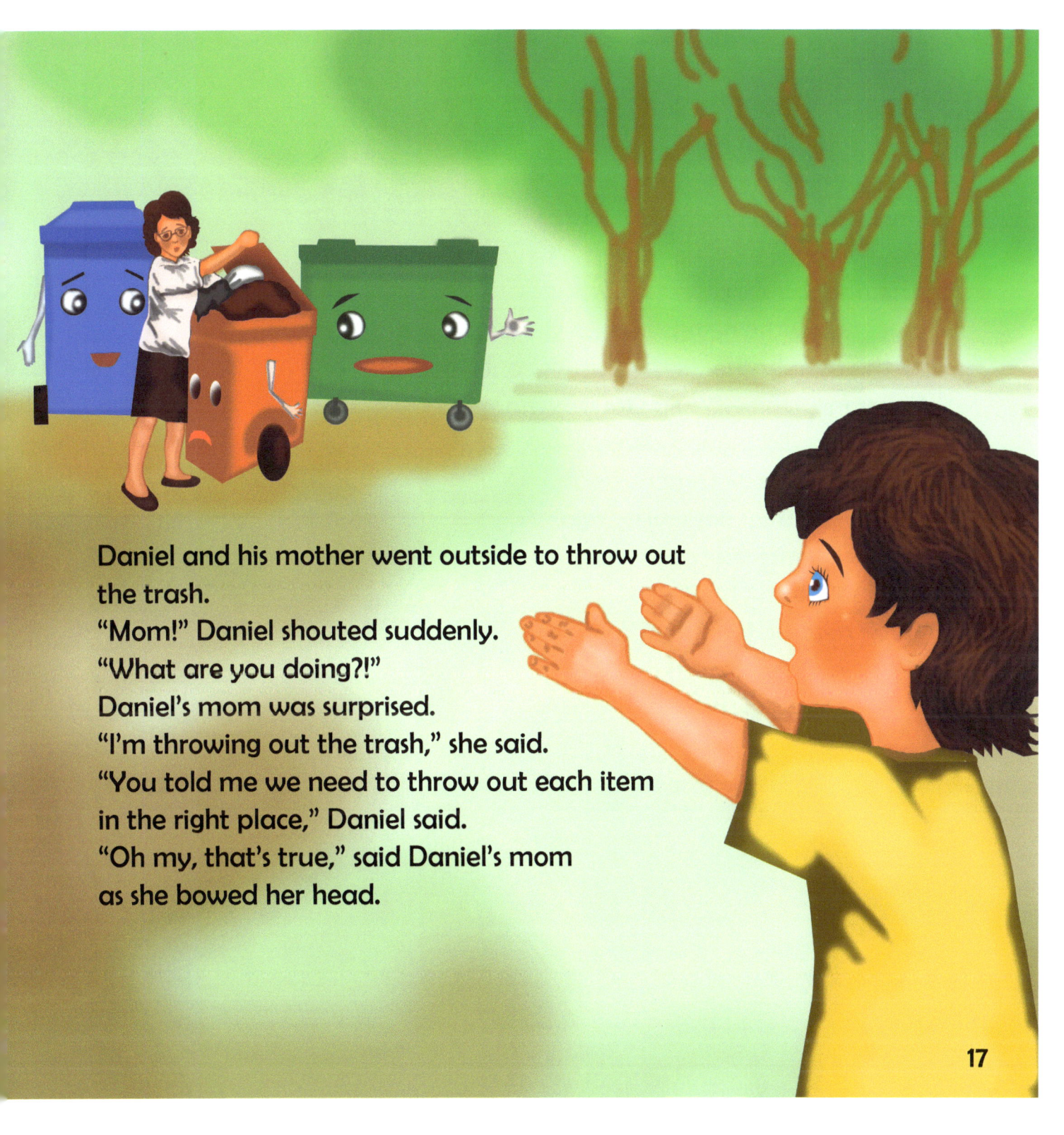

Daniel and his mother went outside to throw out
the trash.
"Mom!" Daniel shouted suddenly.
"What are you doing?!"
Daniel's mom was surprised.
"I'm throwing out the trash," she said.
"You told me we need to throw out each item
in the right place," Daniel said.
"Oh my, that's true," said Daniel's mom
as she bowed her head.

17

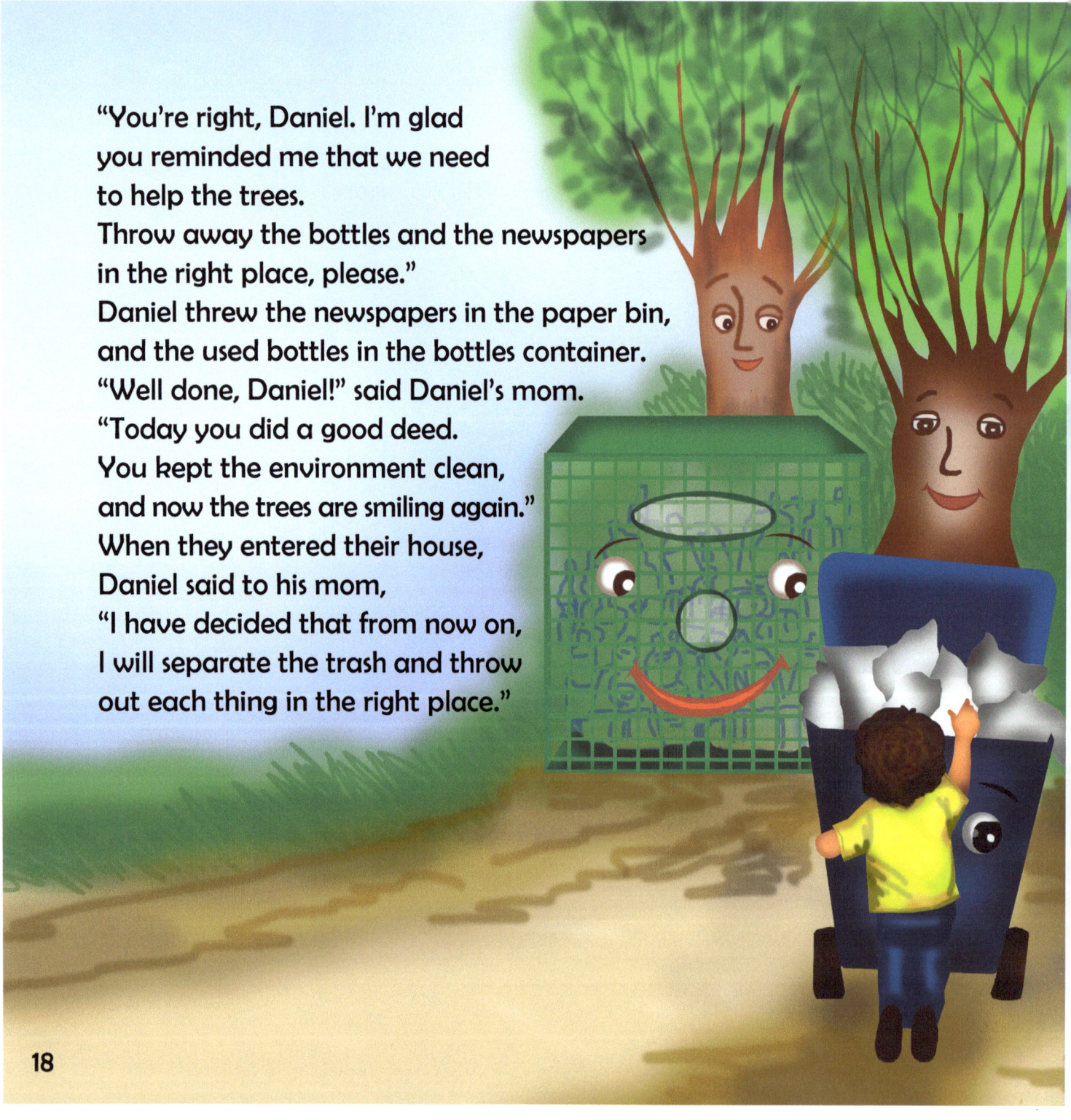

"You're right, Daniel. I'm glad
you reminded me that we need
to help the trees.
Throw away the bottles and the newspapers
in the right place, please."
Daniel threw the newspapers in the paper bin,
and the used bottles in the bottles container.
"Well done, Daniel!" said Daniel's mom.
"Today you did a good deed.
You kept the environment clean,
and now the trees are smiling again."
When they entered their house,
Daniel said to his mom,
"I have decided that from now on,
I will separate the trash and throw
out each thing in the right place."

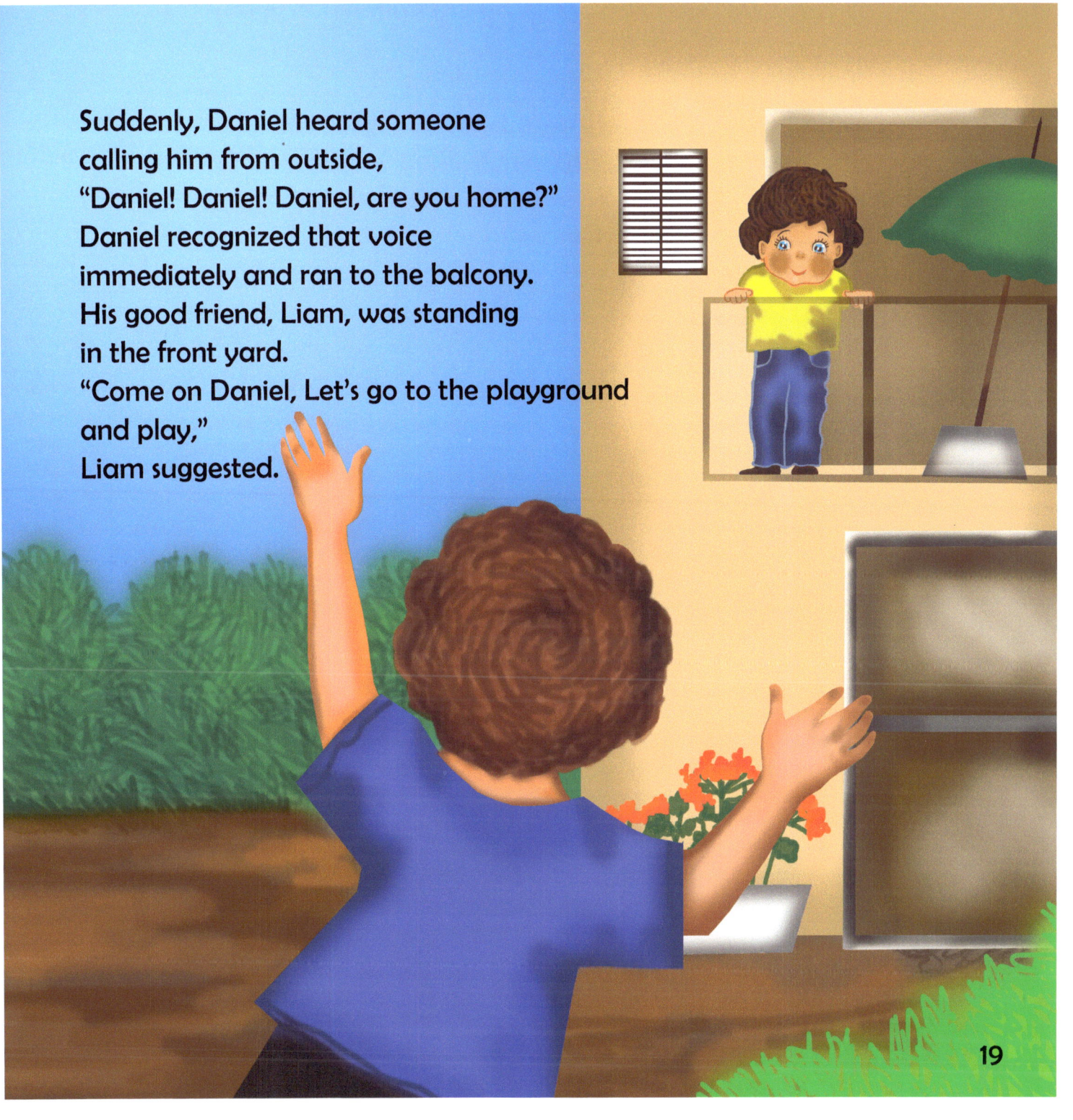

Suddenly, Daniel heard someone
calling him from outside,
"Daniel! Daniel! Daniel, are you home?"
Daniel recognized that voice
immediately and ran to the balcony.
His good friend, Liam, was standing
in the front yard.
"Come on Daniel, Let's go to the playground
and play,"
Liam suggested.

19

Daniel wanted to run outside, but he had to ask his mother first. "Mom, can I play with Liam in the playground?" Daniel asked. "Ok Daniel, but be careful," she said. "Don't go near the road." "We'll be careful!" Daniel promised and ran outside to meet his friend. Many kids from around the neighborhood were playing cheerfully in the playground.

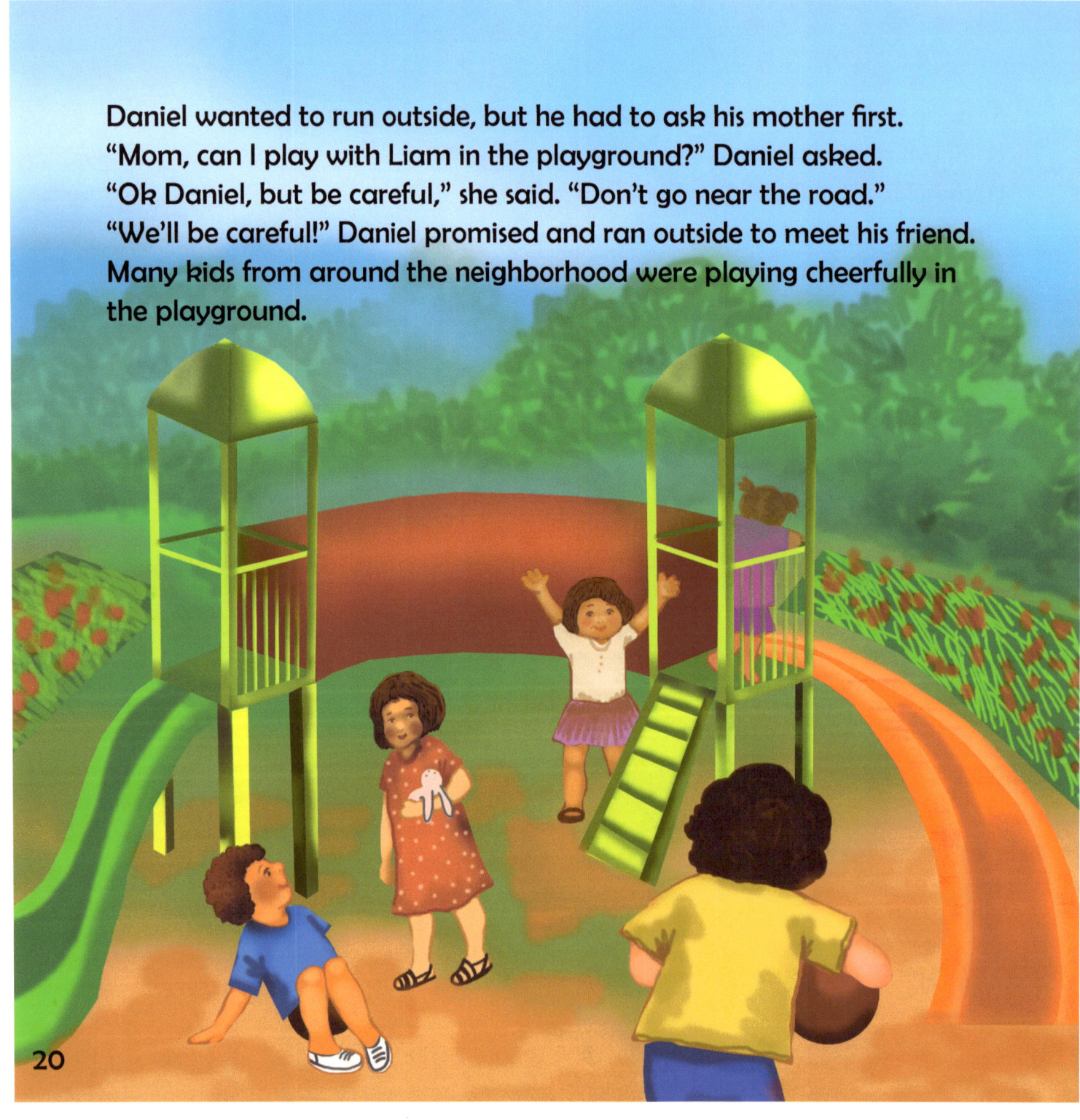

Oliver, the new kid in the neighborhood, was the only one sitting alone.
Daniel approached him. "Oliver, why are you sitting here alone?"
he asked. "Everyone is playing."
"I don't have any friends here
in the neighborhood,"
Oliver said sadly.
"I don't know anybody."

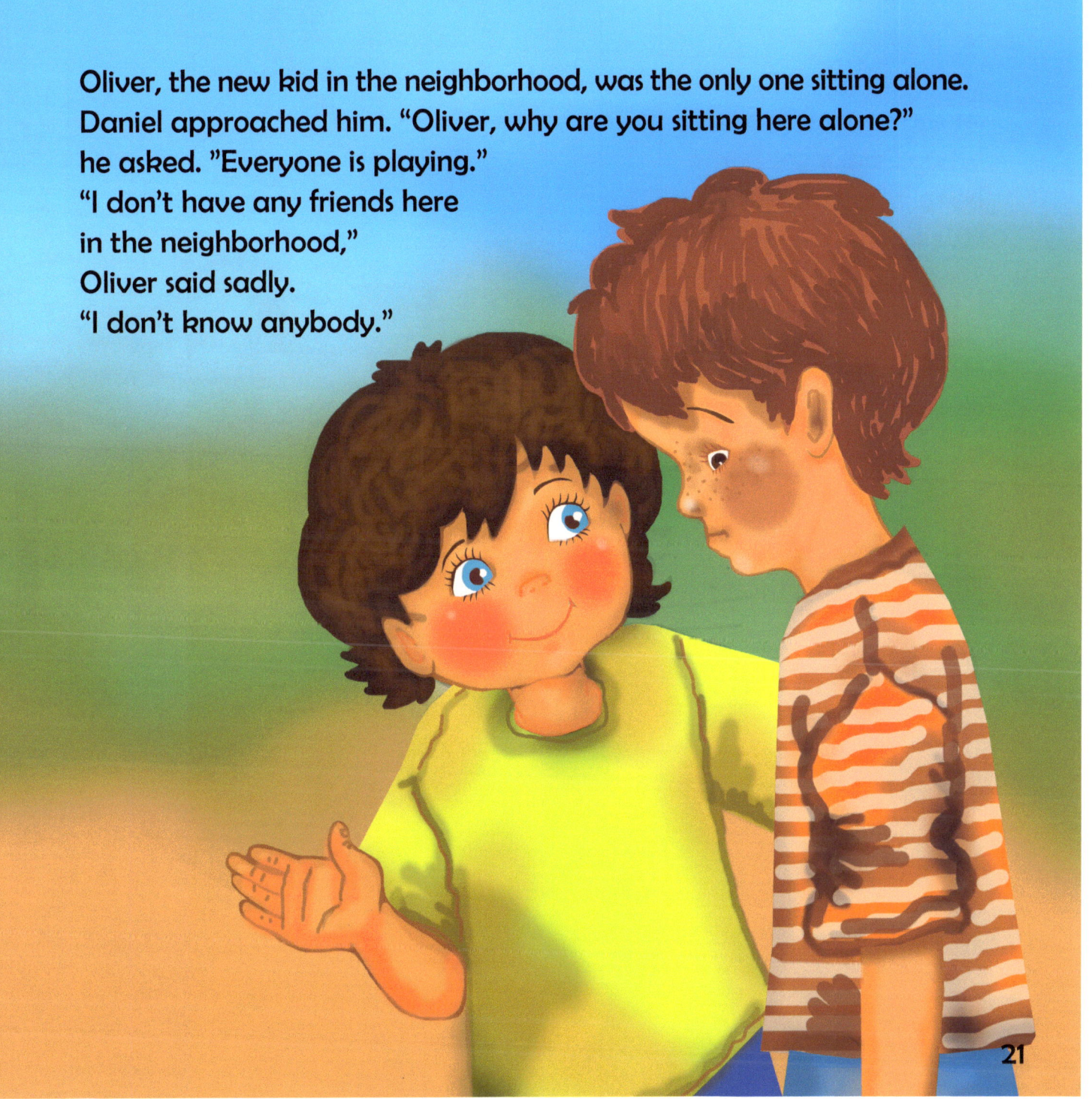

"Come play with us," Daniel said. "We will be your friends."
At that moment, a smile spread across Oliver's face.
When Daniel got home,
he told his mother about Oliver.
"Well done, Daniel," Mom said.
"Today you did a good deed!"

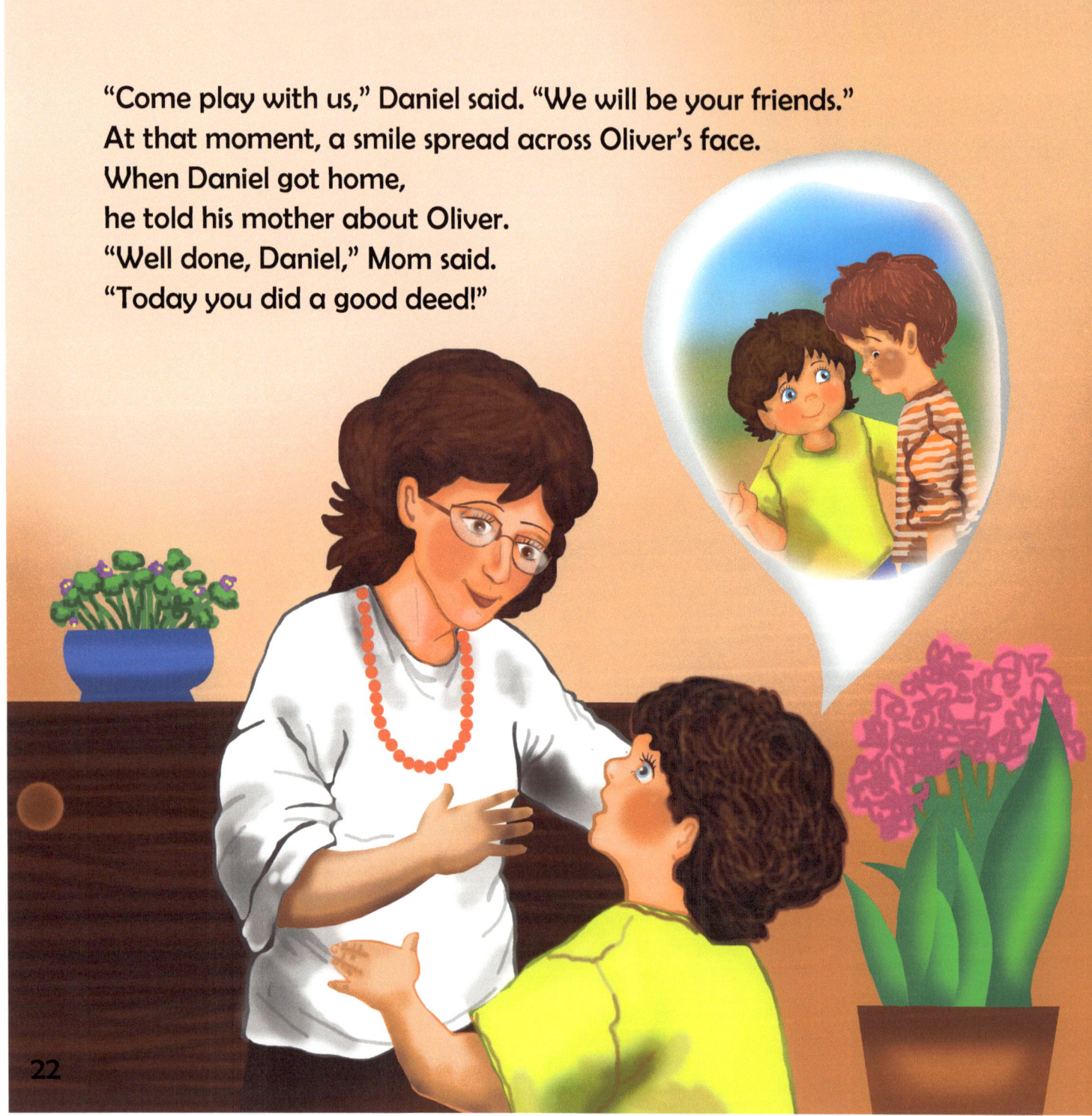

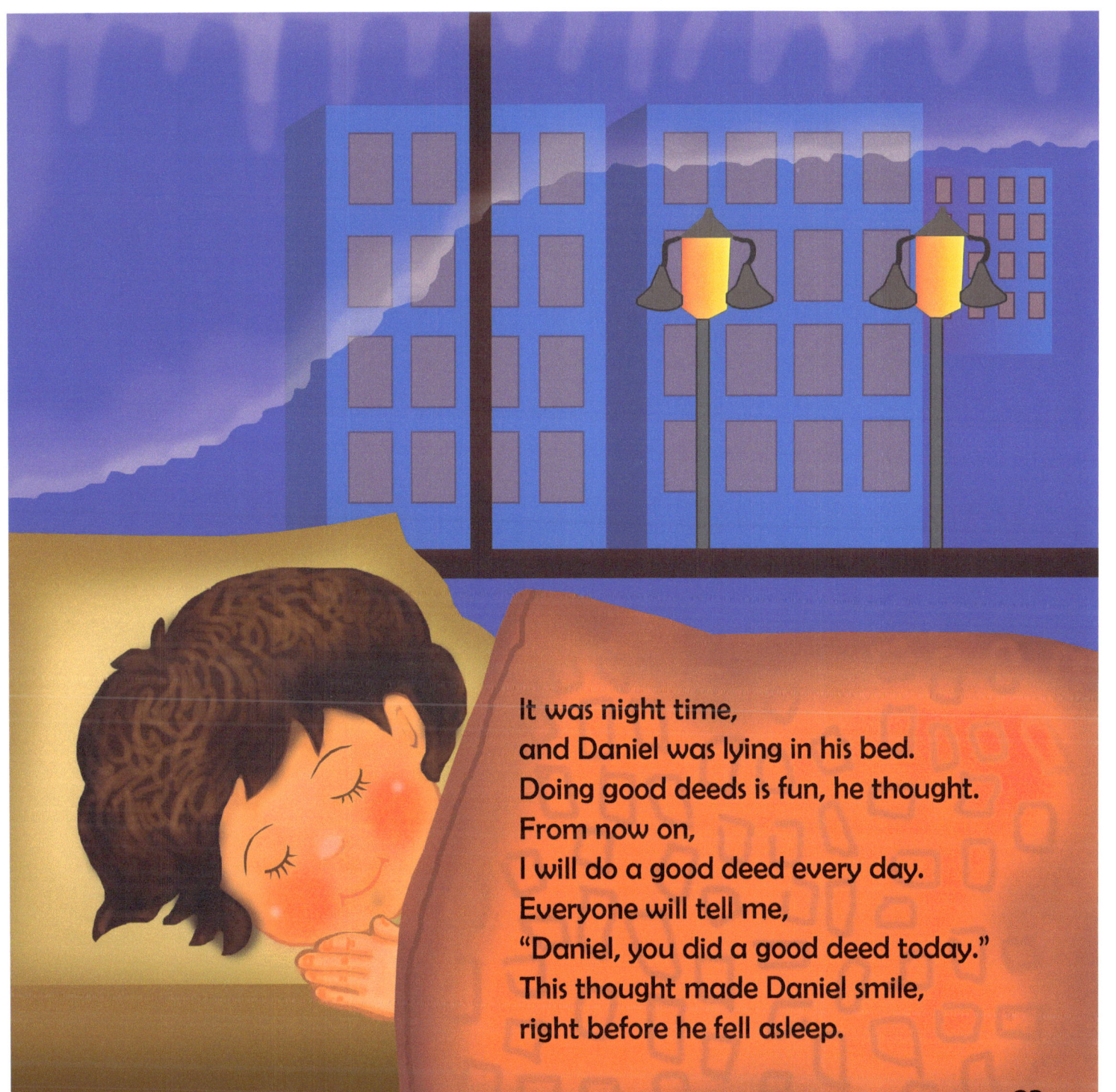

It was night time,
and Daniel was lying in his bed.
Doing good deeds is fun, he thought.
From now on,
I will do a good deed every day.
Everyone will tell me,
"Daniel, you did a good deed today."
This thought made Daniel smile,
right before he fell asleep.

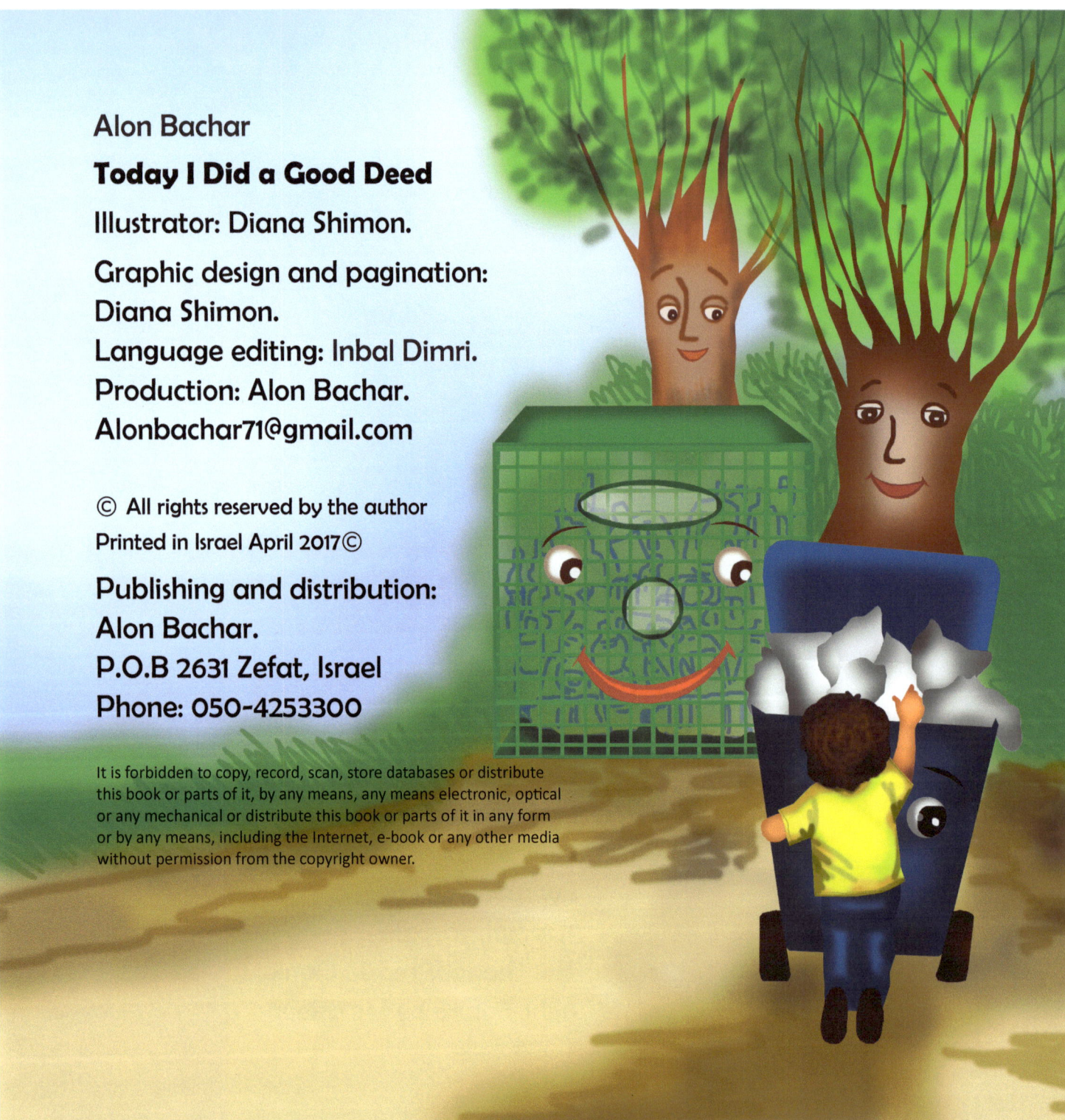

Alon Bachar

Today I Did a Good Deed

Illustrator: Diana Shimon.

Graphic design and pagination:
Diana Shimon.
Language editing: Inbal Dimri.
Production: Alon Bachar.
Alonbachar71@gmail.com

Publishing and distribution:
Alon Bachar.
P.O.B 2631 Zefat, Israel
Phone: 050-4253300

www.ingramcontent.com/pod-product-compliance
Lightning Source LLC
Chambersburg PA
CBHW041308180526
45172CB00003B/1024